MOSAICS

MOSAICS

20 stunning step-by-step projects for the home
and garden, beautifully demonstrated in over
150 practical photographs

HELEN BAIRD

LORENZ BOOKS

This edition is published by Lorenz Books,
an imprint of Anness Publishing Ltd, Hermes House,
88–89 Blackfriars Road, London SE1 8HA;
tel. 020 7401 2077; fax 020 7633 9499
www.lorenzbooks.com; www.annesspublishing.com

If you like the images in this book and would like to investigate
using them for publishing, promotions or advertising, please
visit our website www.practicalpictures.com for information.

UK agent: The Manning Partnership Ltd; tel. 01225 478444;
  fax 01225 478440; sales@manning-partnership.co.uk
UK distributor: Grantham Book Services Ltd; tel. 01476 541080;
  fax 01476 541061; orders@gbs.tbs-ltd.co.uk
North American agent/distributor: National Book Network;
  tel. 301 459 3366; fax 301 429 5746; www.nbnbooks.com
Australian agent/distributor: Pan Macmillan Australia;
  tel. 1300 135 113; fax 1300 135 103;
  customer.service@macmillan.com.au
New Zealand agent/distributor: David Bateman Ltd;
  tel. (09) 415 7664; fax (09) 415 8892

Publisher: Joanna Lorenz
Editorial Director: Helen Sudell
Project Editors: Katy Bevan, Rosie Gordon
Copy Editor: Beverley Jollands
Designers: Adelle Morris and Ian Sandom
Production Controller: Don Campaniello
Additional text: Caroline Suter, Celia Gregory, Mary Maguire,
  Cleo Mussi, Marion Elliot for projects listed below
Photography: Polly Eltes, Debbi Treloar, Rodney Forte,
  Spike Powell, Tim Imrie, Adrian Taylor, Debbie Patterson,
  Zul Mukhida

Projects by Helen Baird, with the following exceptions:
Tessa Brown: love letter rack (pp. 30–1); Victoria Brown:
Mediterranean mirror (pp. 26–7); Marion Elliot: black-and-white tiled
table (pp. 34–5); Sandra Hadfield: funky fruit bowl (pp. 20–1),
windowsill planter (pp. 54–5); Simon Harman: fountain bowl
(pp. 59–61); Mary Maguire: shell table (pp. 56–8); Cleo Mussi: part-
tiled flowerpot (p. 43), plant pots (pp. 44–5), sunflower mosaic (p. 46),
china tiles (pp.50–1), decorative spheres (pp. 52–3); Joanna Nevin:
stained-glass candle holder (pp. 18–19); Sarah Round: house number
plaque (p. 42); Norma Vondee: lemon tree floor (pp. 23–5), sea urchin
garden seat (pp. 62–3).

ETHICAL TRADING POLICY
Because of our ongoing ecological investment programme,
you, as our customer, can have the pleasure and reassurance of
knowing that a tree is being cultivated on your behalf to
naturally replace the materials used to make the book you are
holding. For further information about this scheme, go to
www.annesspublishing.com/trees

© Anness Publishing Ltd 2008

A CIP catalogue record for this book is available from the
British Library.

Previously published as part of a larger volume,
Mosaics by Design

Contents

Getting started

Modern mosaicists work in all manner of styles and bring immense flair to the art. Some draw on traditional influences and ancient techniques, while others break new ground with fresh design, methods and materials. Either approach can produce inspirational mosaic art.

Finding inspiration

Ideas can come from many sources, including nature, animal and plant forms, as well as from the repeating or geometric patterns of Roman, Celtic and Cubist art. The scale of work can vary from small portable panels and accessories to patios and large expanses of floor, as well as murals and immense sculptures. Prolific mosaic makers work on panels, murals and indoor pieces.

Above: This unique mirror complements and enhances the colour scheme in a contemporary home.

Ancient Roman mosaics often included images of the living world. They are mostly realistic, though sometimes they convey a quirky sense of humour. In Byzantine times, mosaic was largely confined to religious or imperial subjects. Forms were made slender, elongated and elegant, and faces became regular and expressionless. It is a style that continues to inspire mosaicists today.

During the 20th century, there was a move towards the abstract in the work of artists such as Picasso, Matisse and Chagall, with the emphasis on outline and colour rather than detail, and the free rendition of line and form. The current revival of interest in mosaic often displays a more naturalistic approach, revelling in the beauty and detail of the natural world.

Above: This image of Neptune and Amphitrite is from a house in Herculaneum and survived a volcano in AD79.

Landscapes

Designs depicting landscapes can, at first glance, appear to be faithful to reality, but most will involve a certain amount of stylization, of tidying up, of selecting particular subjects for the foreground and background, of highlighting details and of trying to create a feeling of distance and three-dimensional space. As with painting, the creation of a landscape begins with the composition. It needs to be planned and sketched out, and the order of work and colours and tones of the tesserae need to be considered in advance.

Images do not have to be naturalistic to be effective. Some contemporary mosaic artists take inspiration from naïve art and the surreal landscapes of artists such as Giorgio de Chirico, and they have produced scenes that make full use of mosaic's textural and graphic qualities. Such works suggest a complete landscape rather than showing highly detailed images and objects.

Plants

Natural plant forms are a very popular theme in mosaic, and plants are often woven into the designs of mosaic borders. They can flow around a panel or large mural, creating wonderful rhythm and activity. Plants and flowers are also excellent individual images, perhaps best for table tops and panels. Trees, especially the tree of life, are a common theme in mosaic.

Marine life

Many mosaic materials, especially the intensely coloured and vibrant material smalti, are wonderful for recreating the many beautiful colours of fish and all the subtle shades of the ocean – azure, emerald, turquoise and aquamarine. Marine themes offer some wonderful opportunities for mosaic artists to experiment with exciting and vivid colour. The impression of water, light and movement can be conveyed effectively and with surprising economy in the way in which the tesserae are laid. Artists can also intersperse the mosaic with iridescent and reflective materials, such as mirror, to highlight certain areas and create a glistening scene.

Below: A strong colour used against a light background stands out more clearly than white on a coloured background, emphasizing the natural curves found in nature.

Animals and people

Living creatures may be treated as symbolic in mosaic, or can be allegorical or humorous, realistic or naturalistic. Unusual materials can be added to give depth, or a strong, two-dimensional outline also works well.

The depiction of the human form can be realistic, as in Roman examples, or more abstract. Figurative mosaic in the hands of an expert may display great detail and intricacy. In such mosaics, the tesserae are cut to size and positioned for their shape – notably to show the jut of the chin, cheekbones and brow. Tesserae are carefully chosen to suggest gradations of colour and tone and to show the way light and shade fall on the face or body.

Left: Echoes of the art of Paul Klee are visible in this geometric birdbath in tones of blue. The grid effect is offset by the changes in colour.

Planning projects

Collect any pictures or images in books, magazines and other sources that grab your attention and keep them for reference later. The initial drawing will be only a guideline for your mosaic. Keep it simple and clear, with strong lines. If you cannot draw, trace the image or cut out a photocopy, and try out different colour schemes before buying the tiles. If the task is site-specific, it's important to make an accurate template using graph paper or brown paper and/or take measurements before you start the detailed planning and work.

If you are a beginner, it is best to start with a small project so that you can try out the basic techniques. As you become more confident, you can be more ambitious and explore your creativity.

Geometric and abstract patterns

By their nature, geometric patterns are very well suited to the art of mosaic. The basic outlines are simple and ideal for the shape of tesserae, and shapes can be repeated as often as is needed. The repetition is not monotonous: quite the opposite. The effect can be soothing and pleasing to the eye, and variations can be achieved through different colourways. A repeated pattern is an effective way of linking spaces: for instance, a garden path and hall floor could both be in a simple chequerboard pattern, the path in, say, black and white, and the hallway in blue and white.

There are many classic patterns to choose from, such as the Greek key, Celtic designs or the sinuous calligraphic motifs of Islamic or Arabic art. Geometric shapes often occur in 20th-century art, and Mondrian's blocks of colour, for example, would translate well into a mosaic project.

Creating a workspace

While a small project could be made in the kitchen, it is advisable to allocate a special space in which to work, giving you a clean area for drawing and a workbench or table for doing the mosaic.

Posture

The most comfortable way to work is definitely at a table or easel. It is important to have your stool or seat at the right height. If you are working on a mosaic that is too big for a table or easel, you should work on, or at least prepare the design on, the floor. You will need a hard surface, so if the floor is carpeted, cover it with a large piece of wood. If you are using the indirect method, you should draw up the design and get a clear understanding of the whole image. Then you can cut the image into fragments and work in sections on the table.

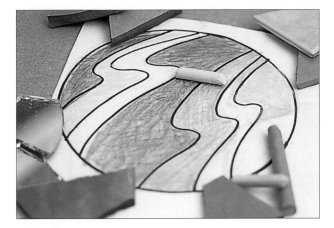

Left: It is useful to make a simple line drawing first using a soft pencil, then emphasize the lines with a black pen and shade in the colours you intend to use.

Lighting

Ideally your table or workbench should be placed near a source of natural light. Daylight is the best way to see true colour. When light is limited or you are working in the evening, daylight bulbs are ideal. Have more than one light source if possible, to avoid shadows.

Storage

It is a good idea to store tiles in glass or clear plastic jars, so it is easy to see how much stock you have. Tools are expensive and rust easily, so keep them clean and dry. Adhesives and grouts solidify if they get wet, so they must all be stored in a damp-free area.

Preparing for work

Gather all the required tools and materials together, mix enough fixing agents for the immediate work and lay out a good range of tiles before you start. Keep your work area clean, sweeping away loose fragments regularly. When you are working with cement-based adhesive, clean any excess off while it is damp, as it will harden if left for several hours and become difficult to remove. Avoid pouring any adhesive or grout down the drain, as they may cause blockages.

Safety
- Wear goggles when cutting materials.
- Wear a face mask when cutting wood or mixing powders.
- Wear hardwearing gloves when cutting wire and use rubber or latex gloves when mixing up powders, and also when grouting, cleaning or sculpting.
- Hold mosaic tile nippers at the far end of the handle to avoid blistering your hands.
- Clean and vacuum the work area regularly to avoid an unnecessary build-up of dust.
- Create your mosaic with awareness of the safety of those around you, as well as yourself.

Below: You may need to use the floor for planning, as below, but a a desk and chair that promote good posture are essential for your fine detail work, as is plenty of light.

Planning a Design

The wide choice of materials available means that designing a mosaic is a highly personal process. You need to consider such aspects as size, location, use and colour before starting work.

Permanence

Your designs should take into account the fact that mosaic is long-lasting and the colours are virtually permanent. Once the setting medium is hard, changes cannot be made. These qualities are the great strengths of mosaic, but they also mean you cannot go over your work and cover it up. All you need to do is be clear about what you want to achieve and how you want to realize it. Do your planning well, and materials, colour and style will marry happily with setting, mood and size to give you a mosaic of which you are proud.

Above: The choice of white or dark grouting will affect the overall appearance of the mosaic.

Points to consider for interiors
- What is the mosaic's function?
- Which room is it going in?
- Is the room's colour scheme being built around the mosaic?
- If not, does the mosaic fit with the existing scheme?
- Is the design you are considering appropriate to the room where you intend to place the mosaic?
- Are the weight of the object and the material used appropriate to its function and position?
- What happens if you decide to redecorate?
- Is the mosaic portable ?
- If not, what will happen if you later want to move it to a different place, or you move house?

Points to consider for exteriors
- What is the mosaic for?
- Where is it going to be sited?
- Do you want it to blend in, or will it be the focus from which all else flows?
- Are the colours of the mosaic suitable for its purpose, size and location? If not, can you adjust these to match better?
- Is the mosaic the right size for its specific purpose: not so small that it is lost, nor so big that it dominates the space?
- If it is to convey information, such as a house name or number, is the design uncluttered with detail and clear enough to enable it to be viewed from a distance?

Colour and contrast

When deciding which colours to use, bear in mind the visual effect they will have. A palette of warm colours – reds, oranges and yellows – will create an impression of warmth. Strong tones will dominate the surroundings.

Cool colours – blues, greens and indigos – are effective in making small spaces seem larger. The palette you choose must match the style of the design: for example, a realistic floral mosaic will be most successful if executed in colours as close as possible to the natural plants. You will also need to take into consideration the items that will surround your mosaic. However much you may want it to provide a focal point, it needs to bear some relation to the existing colour scheme in the room, or it will simply look out of place.

An element of contrast adds drama and movement to a design, and is necessary to satisfy the eye and keep it interested. It can be introduced in many different ways, not just in the choice of colour. Mixed-media mosaics create the vital element of contrast simply through their mixture of materials. Varying the sizes and shapes of the tiles within patterns and in different areas of the design is another way of creating contrast. Using just black and white provides the most extreme colour contrast, but shades of the same colour, or a palette of related tones, can be just as effective.

A touch of the unexpected works well: a matt chequerboard in black and white can be transformed by silver or glass tesserae placed at random intervals, while a pebble pool surround may be brought to life with a few beautifully shaped shells.

Shape and form

You can create almost any pattern or shape you want with mosaic, once you have some experience of cutting and working with the medium. If you are a beginner, it is best to use broad outline rather than fine detail – you need to get used to your materials and the effects they can make.

Right: You can create wonderful patterns with square tesserae. The lines in this piece are laid out in curves, which gives a great sense of movement.

To start with, you could study the work of cartoonists, who evoke people, places and whole landscapes with a few lines, and it is worth experimenting with this "less is more" principle when planning your design.

Laying the tesserae to form images and patterns is an essential element of mosaic. The art lies in laying the lines of tesserae to flow around a subject or group to create rhythm and movement, or to flow in directional lines, leading towards or around a design.

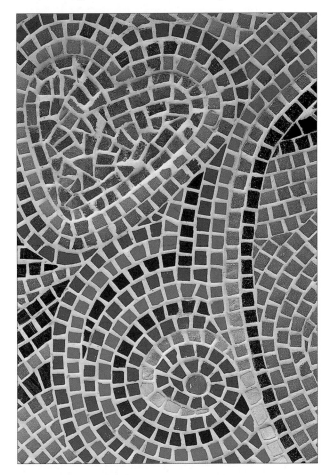

Choosing Materials

The tesserae you use need to be suitable in style and scale for your mosaic and its position. They should not be too large to cope with the detail, or so small that they weaken its impact.

Marble, smalti and gold leaf

In Graeco-Roman times marble was used, and it is still associated with beauty and natural elegance. It has a depth and timeless quality beyond any other material. The colours are soft and the variations in tone are subtle: white, chalky pinks and rose, through to delicate greens, blues and blacks. Polishing intensifes the colours. For use in mosaics, marble is generally cut from rods with a hammer and hardie (a type of anvil). You can also buy marble that has been machine-cut into regular squares laid on to a paper backing: this is a cheaper form that can be used to cover large areas quickly.

Smalti is opaque glass, and is available in a great variety of colours. Mosaics made from smalti characteristically have a slightly uneven surface, which creates a brilliant reflective quality. This bumpiness means that smalti mosaics are often butted together and left ungrouted, so they cannot be used on floors.

Gold leaf is the most opulent material available to the mosaicist. It is expensive, but it can be used sparsely in a mosaic and still have a great impact and effect. The tesserae have a backing glass, which is usually turquoise, yellow or green. Then there is a layer of 24-carat gold leaf, which is protected with a thin layer of clear or coloured glass. Other variations are available, using silver or copper leaf, a thin film of gold alloy or other metals.

Ceramic and glass tiles

Vitreous glass is cheaper and more accessible than smalti. It comes in sheets, which can be used whole to cover large areas or split into sections or individual pieces. Cutting the individual tiles into four creates the classic square tesserae; the glass is easy to clip and offers extensive potential for intricate design. Glass tiles can be shiny, round, square, bumpy, thick, thin, smooth or textured, and come in many different colours.

Above: Smalti is opaque and creates a great texture.
Above, right: Marble can be hand cut from slabs.

Above: Marble may come ready-cut, in sheets.
Above, right: A huge variety of ceramic tiles is available.

Ceramic tiles: Mosaic ceramic tesserae can be round or square and are made from porcelain. They are good for creating texture, as they are available both glazed and unglazed: using a combination of the two can add surface interest. The colour is uniform in unglazed tiles, and the surface is likely to be matt and more porous than that of glazed tiles. Ceramic tiles are inexpensive and widely available.

Household tiles: Glazes on ordinary household tiles can be very glossy, and this enables you to play with the reflection of light in the design. When smashed up into irregular shapes, they are good for working into abstract designs. They offer enormous variety and versatility to the mosaic artist, and it is possible to cover large areas cheaply with them.

China fragments

A mosaic created with broken china is a wonderful way to recycle old pieces that are pretty but no longer usable, and is completely individual, because no two pieces are likely to be the same. China and crockery are not suitable for intricate designs, but can create wonderful patterns and texture. Odd pieces of pottery with quirky handles, lids and patterns can add some humour to a mosaic.

Mirror

You can buy mirror in sheets made up of small squares or rectangles, or in large sheets that need to be smashed up. Mirror works very well scattered through a coloured mosaic. It also produces a fantastic effect when covering entire surfaces, especially sculpted forms. You can generally get offcuts from a glazier for little or nothing.

Stained glass

Coloured glass has a wonderful shimmering quality to it, rather like beautiful jewels. There is even a stained glass that is iridescent and reflects light like mother-of-pearl.

Above: Storing tiles in glass jars is a colourful and practical way to see what you have in stock.

Some types of stained glass are pieces of art in themselves. They can be used to cover whole surfaces for a luxurious finish or used in small areas to highlight details in a picture or an abstract pattern. Adding stained glass to a mosaic design will create something special.

Mixed media

A mixture of materials can be particularly effective in sculptural mosaics and for creating a variety of textures and depth in two-dimensional work. It is fun to gather a collection, such as antique beads and costume jewellery, shells, pieces of sea-worn glass or pebbles from garden suppliers. There are no boundaries to what can be used, and it can be challenging to experiment with new methods and a variety of new materials.

Techniques

Before you begin any project, practise cutting, grouting and fixing on scrap tiles. Specialist equipment helps, but practice is essential.

Sheet mosaic

Many mosaic tiles are supplied on sheets. When you are making smaller pieces using sheet mosaic, you should take the tiles off their backing. To remove the tiles from sheets formed with brown paper or mesh, soak the whole sheet in clean warm water. When the glue has dissolved, the tiles will slip off the backing material easily.

Clipping tiles

Mosaic nippers should be held at the end of the handles for the best possible leverage when shaping the edges of tiles. The rounded side of the head is placed over the tile, which need be inserted only a few millimetres. To cut tiles in half, the nippers are positioned in the centre of the tile with the head pointing in the direction in which the cut is to be made. Goggles are essential.

Cutting and sawing tiles

A hand tile cutter is traditionally used for cutting tiles, and it is available from do-it-yourself stores. It will cut straight lines, though its use is limited to ceramic tiles with a soft clay base. Hard porcelain tiles or stone need to be cut with a wet tile saw, which cuts the material with a metal disc turned by a motor and kept cool with water.

Cutting glass

A glass cutter is used for straight lines or large shapes in stained glass and mirror. The surface should first be scored lightly, then the ball of the cutter is used to tap the underside of the glass, which cracks along the line.

Above: A hammer and hardie break thick materials into pieces. Tile cutters can nibble away for finer shapes.

Bases

Unless you are covering a sculpted form, you should work on a flat, even surface for a professional-quality mosaic. Uneven surfaces should be sanded down. Wood needs to be primed. If the base is cement, a new surface should be laid; self-levelling cement is an easy option. The base must be rigid. For example, floorboards are flexible, and a mosaic laid on them will lift if there is movement.

Fixing methods

The direct method involves simply sticking the tesserae, face up, on to the base, which has been covered with a layer of cement-based tile adhesive.

In the indirect method the mosaic is created off-site, then installed. A wooden frame is made to the size of the finished slab, and greased internally with petroleum jelly.

The mosaic is applied to brown paper marked with the dimensions of the slab. When the tesserae have dried, the frame is placed over the paper and dry sand sprinkled over the design and brushed into the crevices. The frame is then filled with mortar. The surface is smoothed, then covered with damp newspaper and plastic sheeting and left to dry slowly for five to six days. The slab and frame are turned over and the brown paper dampened with a wet sponge, then peeled away. The frame is unscrewed and the slab removed.

Adhesives and grouting

Cement-based tile adhesives can be used for both direct and indirect mosaics. Flexible additives can give extra protection against movement or moisture. Medium-strength adhesive is available ready-mixed and is fine for decorative pieces that do not need to be waterproof. You can also use PVA (white) glue to stick tesserae to wood, or two-part epoxy resin glue for damp locations.

Grout comes either ready-mixed or as a powder and in a variety of colours. There are also powdered stains that you can add to create almost any colour you want. The grout should be applied when the tile adhesive is dry. Ensure that the mosaic is clean. Apply the grout over the mosaic, using your fingers (wearing gloves) or a grout spreader. Push the paste into the gaps and smooth it evenly over the whole surface. Wipe away excess grout with a damp sponge. After 10 minutes, further excess grout can be rubbed away easily with a dry cloth. (If left much longer, remove with a nailbrush or paint scraper.) On a large-scale project, the whole surface should not be grouted in one go, because when you start to clean off the grout, the first areas may have already dried.

Finishing

Stone and pebbles look richer when sealed. Sealants come in matt or shiny varieties. Beeswax can be rubbed on to matt tiles to give them a deeper colour, and terracotta tiles need to be treated with linseed oil. Decorative mosaics should be dusted and cleaned using glass cleaner and a dry cloth.

Above: Polish mosaic with a clean dry cloth, preferably a lint-free one, and you should achieve a good shine on glass and glazed ceramic tiles.

INDOORS

Any room can benefit from mosaic design, whether the space is modern or traditional in décor, minimalist, or cluttered and cosy. In this chapter, designs include plant pots, mirrors and even a Mediterranean-style floor, all perfect for bringing light, colour and texture into your home.

Pencil
Ruler
Graph paper
Coloured glass
in several colours
Glass cutter
Pliers
Straight-sided glass jar or
candle holder
Clear adhesive
Flexible knife
Tile grout
Sponge or soft cloth
Nailbrush

Stained-glass Candle Holder

Squares of coloured glass cast beautiful patterns at night, when the candle is lit in a darkened room. Practise the glass-cutting technique first on scraps of clear glass.

STEP 1

STEP 2

STEP 3

1 Draw a grid of 4cm (1½in) squares on graph paper. This is your template.

2 Place each sheet of glass over the grid. Following your drawn lines, score vertical lines down the sheet using a glass cutter.

3 Using pliers, snap the glass along the scored lines into neat, evenly sized strips. Place each strip of glass over the paper grid, and score horizontal lines across.

4 Snap off the squares with the pliers, until you have clipped enough squares in different colours to cover the candle holder.

5 Stick the squares of glass in neat rows around the candle holder with clear adhesive, alternating the colours, and leaving a tiny gap between each tile.

6 Using a flexible knife, spread the tile grout over the mosaic, filling all the gaps.

Quick Tip
Make sure that you leave an even gap between all the tiles and don't push them together as you touch them, as this may spoil the neat regularity of the mosaic's design.

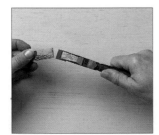

STEP 4

STEP 5

7 Rub the excess grout off with a damp sponge or soft cloth. Leave to dry, and brush off any grout residue with a nailbrush before polishing with a dry cloth. Ensure it has set before using.

Funky Fruit Bowl

In this unusual modern design, the coloured grout forms a major feature, with untiled areas left to show it off. Within the design, the tesserae appear as separate decorative elements, rather than parts of a whole, but there is still a pleasing regular pattern.

STEP 1

STEP 2

STEP 3

1 Using a soft pencil, draw freehand spirals on the outside of the bowl, as shown. Each spiral should be about the same depth as the bowl. Mark a row of triangles along the edges of each spiral.

2 Use tile nippers to cut the glass tiles into small, equal-sized triangles, to fit those drawn on the bowl. Place a blob of PVA (white) glue on each pencilled triangle.

3 Press on a glass triangle. Hold each tessera in place until it sticks.

4 Using tile nippers, cut the white ceramic tiles into large triangles of equal size.

5 Apply a thick layer of glue over the inside of the bowl and over the back of each triangle. Press the triangles in place, leaving large gaps between them.

STEP 4

STEP 5

STEP 6

6 Dot small blobs of PVA glue at regular intervals around the bowl's rim and press on the glass nuggets firmly, alternating the colours. Leave the glue to dry overnight.

STEP 7

STEP 8

STEP 9

STEP 10

7 Mix the fabric stain with water following the manufacturer's instructions. You can choose any of the many colours available, to go with the mosaic.

8 Gradually add the stain to the tile grout and mix thoroughly. The final colour of the dried grout will be slightly lighter than its colour when wet.

9 Using a rubber spreader, spread the coloured grout over the entire bowl, evening out the surface. Gently smooth it all over the bowl with your hands. Wipe off the excess grout with a damp sponge. Leave to dry for 1 hour.

10 Polish the surface of the bowl with a dry, soft cloth, removing any residual grout.

YOU WILL NEED
12mm (½in) thick chipboard
(particle board),
30 x 30cm (12 x 12in)
Pencil
Ruler
PVA (white) glue
Paintbrush
Jigsaw (saber saw)
Abrasive paper (sandpaper)
Tile nippers
Ceramic household tiles:
yellow, dark blue and lilac
Mirror
Tile adhesive
Flexible knife
Sponge
Black grout
Grout spreader
Felt
Scissors
Soft cloth
Clear glass polish

Pot Stand

As well as protecting your table top, this mosaic pot stand will brighten up any kitchen table. The geometric shape is integral to the pattern in which the tesserae are laid. Here, small pieces of mirror have been added to the dark areas, and small pieces of the dark tiles have been included in the lighter sections.

1 Carefully draw the shape of the pot stand on to the piece of chipboard (particle board); use a ruler to make sure the lines are straight. Prime both sides of the chipboard with diluted PVA (white) glue and leave to dry.

2 Cut around the edge of the shape using a jigsaw (saber saw). Sand down any rough edges and prime with diluted PVA glue. Leave to dry.

3 Draw a design on the stand and, using tile nippers, cut the tiles and mirror into small pieces to fit. Fix them in position with tile adhesive, using a flexible knife. When the surface is covered, sponge off excess adhesive and leave to dry for 24 hours.

4 Fill the gaps with black grout. Rub grout into the sides of the stand, then leave to dry for 10 minutes. Sponge off excess grout, then leave to dry for 24 hours.

5 Paint the sides with diluted PVA glue. Cut a piece of felt to size and stick it to the base with PVA glue. Finish by polishing the top with a soft cloth and a few sprays of clear glass polish.

STEP 1

STEP 3

STEP 5

Lemon Tree Floor

This lovely design is inspired by the tiled floors in Mediterranean countries. The finished mosaic is covered with a sheet of sticky-back plastic and lowered on to the floor in sections.

STEP 1

STEP 2

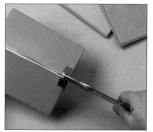
STEP 3

1 Draw sufficient lemon and leaf shapes on sheets of different coloured papers to cover the area of floor you wish to mosaic. Cut out the leaves and lemons and arrange them on the sheet of white paper.

2 When you are happy with the design, draw in details such as stems and a decorative border around the edge of the design, using a felt-tipped pen. Do not try to be over-detailed.

3 Using a tile cutter, score and break all the coloured ceramic household tiles down the centre. Cut each half again down its length, to make strips.

4 Using tile nippers, cut the tile pieces into small, equal-sized tesserae. Cut up the china and some of the black mosaic tiles to outline each lemon, again into pieces of equal size. Following your paper design, arrange the pieces on a flat surface.

Quick Tip
Break each tile into neat halves by applying equal pressure on either side of the scored line with the tile cutter. This should result in a clean break, but you may need some spares.

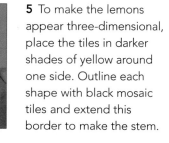
STEP 4

STEP 5

5 To make the lemons appear three-dimensional, place the tiles in darker shades of yellow around one side. Outline each shape with black mosaic tiles and extend this border to make the stem. ▶

STEP 6

STEP 7

STEP 8

6 Using tile nippers, cut the white glazed tiles into random shapes. Fill in the background with a mosaic of large and small pieces.

7 When a section of the design is complete, hold the pieces together with a sheet of sticky-back plastic (contact paper). Peel the backing paper off the plastic and lay it carefully over the loose mosaic.

8 Smooth your hands gently over the plastic sheet to make sure it has stuck securely to all the tesserae and that any air bubbles are eliminated.

9 Finish with a border. This undulating border is made of square, yellow tesserae, outlined with rectangular black tiles.

10 Using a craft (utility) knife, cut through the plastic to separate the mosaic into manageable sections.

11 Spread tile adhesive over the floor area, using a notched spreader. Lower the mosaic carefully into the tile adhesive, section by section.

12 Press the mosaic down firmly so that the surface is flat and even and leave to dry overnight.

13 When the adhesive is dry, peel off the plastic sheet then grout the mosaic with more tile adhesive, using a rubber spreader. Wipe off any excess adhesive immediately using a damp sponge. Leave to dry, then polish with a dry, soft cloth.

STEP 9

STEP 10

STEP 11

Aquatic Mirror

Small blue and gold mosaic tiles make an attractive frame inspired by the colours of the sea. To keep the project neat and simple, plan the dimensions of the frame to suit the size of the tiles: this way you can avoid having to cut and fit odd-shaped pieces.

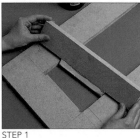
STEP 1

STEP 2

STEP 3

1 Draw a rectangular frame on MDF (medium-density fiberboard). Cut it out using a saw. Drill corner holes for the centre and cut this out with a jigsaw (saber saw). Cut out a shelf, leaving a tab to fit the lower lip of the frame, and glue it to the frame with wood glue. Allow to dry.

2 Prime both sides of the frame and the shelf with white acrylic primer to seal it. Allow to dry. Apply tile adhesive to a small area of the frame, using the fine-notched side of a grout spreader.

3 Apply a random selection of tiles, leaving 2mm (¹⁄₁₆in) gaps between them. Complete the frame, working on a small area at a time. Tile the edges with a single row of tiles.

4 Allow the tile adhesive to dry overnight. Wearing rubber (latex) gloves, spread grout over the surface of the tiles with the spreader. Next, scrape off the excess with the spreader and clean off any remaining grout with a soft cloth. Leave to dry thoroughly.

5 Position the mirror face down on the back of the frame and secure it with narrow frame moulding, glued in place on the back of the frame with wood glue. Allow to dry.

6 Screw two ring screws in place on the back of the mirror frame, more than halfway up the sides towards the top, and tie on a length of picture wire securely, to hang it on a wall.

Country Cottage Tray

This design is simple to execute and adds a naïve charm to a plain wooden tray. The semi-indirect method of laying the tiles used here helps to keep the surface of the mosaic smooth and flat.

STEP 1

STEP 2

STEP 5

1 Cut a piece of brown paper to fit the bottom of the wooden tray. Draw a country cottage scene in pencil on the paper. Plan the colour scheme for the picture, then, using tile nippers, cut all the vitreous glass tiles into quarters.

2 Position the tesserae on the paper to check your design before going further. Once you are satisfied with the design, apply water-soluble glue to the paper in small areas, and stick the tesserae on, face down. Trim the tesserae to fit if necessary.

3 Prepare the tray base by removing any varnish or polish with white spirit (paint thinner). Prime with diluted PVA (white) glue, leave it to dry, then score it with a sharp instrument such as a bradawl. Protect the sides with masking tape.

4 Spread an even layer of tile adhesive over the bottom of the tray, using a notched spreader. Cover the tray completely and spread the adhesive well into the corners.

5 Place the mosaic carefully on the freshly applied tile adhesive, paper side up. Press down firmly over the whole surface, then leave for about 30 minutes. Moisten the paper with a damp sponge and peel off. Leave the tile adhesive to dry overnight.

6 Some parts of the mosaic may need to be grouted with extra tile adhesive. Leave it to dry, then clean off any of the adhesive that may have dried on the surface with a sponge. Remove the pieces of masking tape and then polish the mosaic with a dry, soft cloth.

YOU WILL NEED
3mm (⅛in) and 12mm (½in)
thick MDF
(medium-density fiberboard)
or plywood sheet
Pencil
Jigsaw (saber saw)
PVA (white) glue
Paintbrushes
Wood glue
Panel pins (brads)
Pin hammer
Vitreous glass mosaic tiles
Tile nippers
White cellulose filler (spackle)
Grout spreader
Sponge
Abrasive paper (sandpaper)
Red acrylic paint

Love Letter Rack

Personal letters and correspondence often have a tendency to be lost or misplaced in a busy household. This simple design for a boldly coloured letter rack could be a decorative solution.

STEP 3

STEP 4

STEP 6

1 Draw the shapes for the front and back pieces on the thinner piece of MDF (medium-density fiberboard) or plywood. Then draw a rectangular base on the thicker piece. Cut out all the pieces with a jigsaw (saber saw).

2 Prime the surfaces with diluted PVA (white) glue. When dry, draw three hearts on to the front panel. Stick the pieces together with wood glue and secure with panel pins (brads).

3 When the glue is dry, select two slightly different tones of red vitreous glass tiles for the heart motifs. Using tile nippers, nibble the tiles into precise shapes to fit your design. Stick the tesserae in position on the front panel of the letter rack using white cellulose filler (spackle).

4 Select the colours of vitreous glass for the background. Trim the tiles to fit snugly around the heart motifs and within the edges of the letter rack. Secure them to the base using cellulose filler, as before, and leave the rack to dry overnight.

5 Smooth more filler over the mosaic using a grout spreader, and rub the filler into all the gaps with your fingers. Rub off any excess filler with a damp sponge and leave to dry.

6 Use abrasive paper (sandpaper) to remove any filler that has dried on the surface of the mosaic, and rub down the edges to neaten them. Paint the edges of the front, and all the surfaces of the letter rack that are not covered with mosaic, with red acrylic paint. Leave to dry.

Jazzy Plant Pot

A plain terracotta pot is decorated with squares of brightly coloured tesserae and mirror glass, set in white tile adhesive. This project is simple but effective – you could decorate several pots in the same range of colours to make a matching set.

STEP 1

STEP 4

STEP 5

1 Paint the inside of the terracotta plant pot with yacht varnish and leave to dry. Cut the glass tiles into neat quarters using tile nippers.

2 Cut small squares of mirror to the same size, also with tile nippers. Continue cutting the tiles until you have enough tesserae, in a variety of colours, to cover the pot completely.

3 Working from the bottom of the pot, spread a thick layer of tile adhesive over a small area at a time using a flexible knife.

4 Press the tesserae into the tile adhesive in rows, starting level with the base and interspersing the coloured glass with the pieces of mirror. Leave to dry overnight.

5 Rub some more tile adhesive all over the surface of the mosaic. Fill any gaps in between the tesserae by working the adhesive into the spaces with a gloved finger, then wipe off the excess adhesive with a damp sponge before it dries. Again, leave to dry overnight.

6 Use abrasive paper (sandpaper) to remove any lumps of tile adhesive that may have dried on to the surface of the tesserae, and to neaten the bottom edge of the pot. Rub down any spots that make the base uneven.

7 Smooth some more tile adhesive all over the rim of the pot. Leave until completely dry, and then polish the finished mosaic with a dry, soft cloth.

Black-and-white Tiled Table

There is something immensely pleasing about the simple regularity of black-and-white patterns, whether the tiles are set chequerboard-style or as diamonds. The border could be thicker, depending on the size of your table, or set in one colour only.

STEP 2

STEP 3

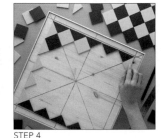

STEP 4

1 Remove the table top and seal with a coat of diluted PVA (white) glue. When the glue has dried, score the surface using a craft (utility) knife.

2 To help you to centre the tiles and work out how wide the borders will be, draw dividing lines (as shown) on the table top.

3 Cut four lengths of wooden batten (furring strip) to fit around the edges of the table. Attach with wood glue and panel pins (brads), leaving a lip around the top edge of exactly the depth of the tiles.

4 Cut a few tiles to make triangles. Lay these out as a border on the table top and fill in with whole tiles to see how many will fit. Draw border lines around the edges.

5 Spread tile adhesive over the surface of the table top, inside the border lines, using a notched spreader.

6 Starting with the triangular border tiles, set out the pattern, butting the tiles together and leaving only very small gaps for the grouting.

7 Cut strips of tile to fit around the borders, then fix in place as before. Once the tiles have dried, grout the surface, working the grout into the gaps and removing any excess with a damp sponge.

8 When the grout is dry, polish the tiles with a dry, soft cloth. Attach the table top to the legs. Seal and paint the table frame and legs if desired.

Splashback Squares

Mosaic is an ideal surface for decorating bathrooms and kitchens since it is waterproof and easy to wipe clean. This simple design is made of tiles in two colours, alternating the colourways in each section to give a chequerboard effect.

STEP 2

STEP 4

STEP 5

1 Prime both sides of the plywood with diluted PVA (white) glue. Leave to dry, then score one side with a bradawl to create a key for the tiles to adhere to.

2 Divide the scored side into eight squares. Draw a simple motif in each.

3 Make a hole in each corner of the plywood, using a bradawl. These will form the holes for the screws to fix the splashback to the wall.

4 Using tile nippers, cut the tiles into random shapes. Following your drawn designs, and using a flexible knife, stick the tiles in place with PVA glue over the pencil markings on each square. Position the tiles carefully around the holes made

for hanging. Wipe off any excess glue with a damp sponge before it dries. Leave until completely dry, preferably overnight.

5 Spread tile adhesive over the surface of the mosaic with a grout spreader or cloth pad, smoothing around the edges with your fingers. Wipe off any excess adhesive and re-open the hanging holes. Leave to dry overnight.

6 Carefully sand off any remaining dried adhesive on the surface of the mosaic. Paint the back of the plywood with yacht varnish to seal it and make it waterproof, and leave to dry for 1–2 hours. Fasten the splashback to the wall with domed mirror screws inserted through the holes at each corner.

YOU WILL NEED
Skirting (base) board
to fit the space
Abrasive paper (sandpaper)
PVA (white) glue
Paintbrush
Soft pencil
Ruler
Piece of sacking (heavy cloth)
Selection of marble tiles
Hammer
Tile adhesive
Flexible knife
Sponge
Soft cloth

Daisy Skirting Board

A skirting board or step riser is an unusual way of introducing mosaic into your home. You can use a repeated design (such as this daisy), a succession of motifs, or a combination of the two.

STEP 2

STEP 4

STEP 5

1 Roughen the surface of the skirting (base) board with coarse-grade abrasive paper (sandpaper), then prime with diluted PVA (white) glue. Leave to dry.

2 Mark the skirting board into small, equally spaced sections. Using a soft pencil, draw a daisy motif in each section.

3 Smash the tiles for the daisies into small pieces with a hammer. It is advisable to wrap them in heavy cloth to do this.

4 Using a flexible knife and working on a small area at a time, spread tile adhesive along the lines of your drawing. Press the pieces of marble firmly into the adhesive. Choose tesserae in shapes that echo the design. The marble can be roughly shaped by tapping the edges of larger tesserae

with a hammer. When each motif is tiled, wipe off any excess adhesive with a sponge and leave to dry overnight.

5 Break up the tiles in the background colour. Working on a small area at a time, spread adhesive on the background and press in the tesserae. When the surface is covered, use small pieces of background colour to tile along the top edge, ensuring that the tesserae do not overlap the edge. Leave to dry for 24 hours.

6 Rub more tile adhesive into the surface, filling all the gaps. Use a flexible knife to spread the adhesive into the edge. Wipe off any excess with a damp sponge and leave overnight to dry. Sand off any dried adhesive on the surface and polish with a dry, soft cloth. Fix in position.

OUTDOORS

From the height of summer, when you
spend so much time in the garden, to
winter, when you need something bold and
colourful to brighten up dull walls or
borders, mosaic can be a great asset.
Opt for practical and decorative plaques or
furniture, or experiment with sculptural
pieces, such as wall mosaics or fountains.

House Number Plaque

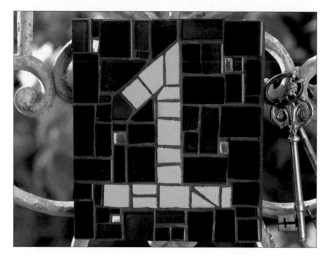

Made with tesserae cut from coloured tiles and fragments of mirror, this plaque should be clearly visible from a distance. A larger plaque could be made in the same way to display a house name.

1 Cut a piece of chipboard (particle board) to size, depending on the length of the house number required. The one used here is 18 x 15cm (7 x 6in). Draw the house number on the chipboard, making each stroke at least 1.5cm (⅝in) wide so it can be seen from a distance. If you wish, you can also mark the intended positions of the pieces of mirror.

2 Paint the chipboard – front, back and sides – with diluted PVA (white) glue. Leave to dry thoroughly.

3 Cut the tiles and mirror into small pieces using tile nippers. First tile the number with the yellow tesserae you have cut, sticking them on the base, a small area at a time, with tile adhesive. Then tile the

area around the number in both shades of blue, cutting and applying small pieces of mirror to the marked positions.

4 Wipe off any excess tile adhesive and leave the plaque to dry for 24 hours.

5 Cover the surface with black tile grout, filling all the gaps between the tesserae so that no moisture will be able to penetrate to the chipboard base. Spread the grout along the edges of the plaque, then leave to dry for about 10 minutes. Sponge off the excess grout and leave to dry for a further 24 hours.

6 Paint the back with exterior paint and fix a clip for hanging. Polish the plaque with a soft cloth and clear glass polish.

YOU WILL NEED
Ready-glazed, high-fired
stoneware flowerpot
Chalk or wax crayon
Selection of china and mirror
Tile nippers
Tile adhesive
Flexible knife
Tile grout
Cement stain
Rubber (latex) gloves
Nailbrush
Soft cloth

Part-tiled Flowerpot

This flowerpot, with its richly-coloured design of stylized flowers, could form a beautiful focal point on the patio or in the garden. Small squares of mirror are incorporated to add reflections.

1 Draw a simple design on the pot, using chalk or a wax crayon. Cut appropriate shapes from the china and mirror using tile nippers. Use tile adhesive to fix the tesserae to the pot, spreading it with a flexible knife. Work first on the main lines and detailed areas, applying the adhesive to just a small area at a time so you can see the design and follow its lines.

2 Fill in the larger areas of the design using tesserae in a plain colour. When these areas are complete, leave the pot to dry for 24 hours.

3 Mix the tile grout with a little cement stain, then spread the grout over the pot with gloved fingers, filling all the cracks between the tesserae. Allow to dry. Brush off excess grout with a nailbrush. After the pot has dried for about 48 hours polish it with a dry, soft cloth.

Quick Tip
If you are using broken china in a mosaic, look out for well-defined motifs that could form focal points in your design. Nibble round them carefully with tile nippers to make satisfying shapes.

YOU WILL NEED

Terracotta plant pots
PVA (white) glue and
brush (optional)
Acrylic paint
Paintbrush
Chalk or wax crayon
Plain and patterned
ceramic tiles
Tile nippers
Rubber (latex) gloves
Tile adhesive
Flexible knife
Tile grout
Cement stain
Cloth
Nailbrush
Soft cloth

Plant Pots

Fragments of plain and patterned broken tiles have been incorporated into the design of these plant pots. Collect your materials by looking for old ceramic tiles in contrasting and complementary colours and patterns.

STEP 1

STEP 2

STEP 3

1 If the plant pots are not frost-resistant and are intended for outdoor use, seal them inside and out with a coat of diluted PVA (white) glue. This will help to keep out any water that might seep into the porous pot, making it vulnerable to frost damage. Allow to dry.

2 Paint the inside of the pots with acrylic paint in your chosen colour. Leave to dry. Using chalk or a wax crayon, roughly sketch out the design for the tile pieces on the unpainted outside of the pot. Keep your designs as simple as possible and in keeping with this small scale.

3 Using tile nippers, snip small pieces of tile to fit within your design. Using a flexible knife, spread tile adhesive on to

small areas of the design at a time. Wearing rubber (latex) gloves, press the tesserae in place, working inside the outlines first, then over the background. Leave for 24 hours to dry.

4 Mix the tile grout with a little cement stain. Spread the grout over the pot with a cloth, filling all the cracks between the tesserae. Wipe off any excess grout. Allow the surface to dry thoroughly.

5 Brush off any dried-on grout with a nailbrush. If there are stubborn parts of grout that will not come off at first, you may need to use wire (steel) wool, a paint scraper or patio cleaner. Allow the mosaic to dry thoroughly for at least 48 hours, then polish with a dry, soft cloth.

Sunflower Mosaic

5mm (¼in) thick
plywood sheet
Pencil
Coping saw or
electric scroll saw
Abrasive paper (sandpaper)
Bradawl
Electric cable
Wire cutters
Masking tape
PVA (white) glue
Paintbrushes
White undercoat
China fragments
Mirror strips
Tile nippers
Tile adhesive
Tile grout
Cement stain
Rubber (latex) gloves
Nailbrush
Soft cloth

This sunflower mosaic is simple to make, and uses cheerful fragments of china in a harmonious blend of colours.

1 Draw a sunflower on the plywood. Cut it out with a saw and sand any rough edges. Make two holes in the plywood with a bradawl. Strip the cable and cut a short length of wire. Push the ends of the wire through the holes from the back and secure the ends with masking tape at the front. Seal the front of the plaque with diluted PVA (white) glue and the back with white undercoat.

2 Using tile nippers, cut the china and mirror strips into irregular shapes. Dip each fragment in the tile adhesive and stick them to the plywood. Scoop up enough of it to cover the sticking surface; the tile adhesive needs to squelch out around the edge of the mosaic to make sure that it adheres securely. Leave the adhesive to dry thoroughly overnight before you grout the mosaic.

Quick Tip
You could make several sunflowers in different designs and hang them on a fence or wall to create an eye-catching outside feature.

STEP 1

STEP 2

3 Mix some cement stain with the grout and press it into the gaps with gloved fingers. Leave for about 5 minutes, then brush off any excess. Leave for 5 minutes, then polish with a dry cloth. Leave to dry.

Princess Wall Mosaic

Garden settings offer mosaic artists the opportunity to experiment with more playful wall mosaics. This rather tongue-in-cheek princess design uses tesserae of vitreous glass in vibrant colours that will not fade over time.

STEP 1

STEP 2

STEP 3

1 Draw a simple design of a princess on brown paper. This mosaic will be worked using the indirect method, so remember that the design will be reversed and plan your picture accordingly.

2 Make a tracing of the outline of your drawing and cut it out. You will use this later as a template to mark the area of the wall to be covered with tile adhesive.

3 Using tile nippers, cut a number of brown vitreous glass mosaic tiles into eighths. These pieces will be used for the outline of the design.

4 Stick the brown tesserae face down on to the main lines of your drawing using water-soluble glue. Add any key features, such as the eyes and lips, in contrasting colours cut into appropriate shapes.

5 Cut the pink vitreous glass tiles into quarters. Glue these face down to fill in the areas of skin between the outlines. Try to make the lines of tiles follow the contours of the face. ▶

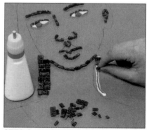
STEP 4

STEP 5

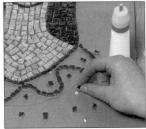

STEP 6

STEP 7

STEP 8

6 Cut the mirror into small pieces about the same size as the quartered vitreous glass tesserae.

7 Stick the pieces of mirror face down on to the dress and in the crown.

8 Cut the tiles for the dress and the crown into quarters and glue them face down between the pieces of mirror. Leave the paper-backed mosaic to dry for 24 hours while securely in position.

9 To transfer the mosaic to its final location, draw around the tracing paper template on the garden wall or floor. Carry the mosaic to the site on a large wooden board to prevent any tesserae coming loose.

Quick Tip
This kind of wall mosaic looks most effective if it is sited where it will peep out between the planting, rather than being in full view from everywhere in the garden.

10 Spread tile adhesive over the whole of the marked area using a notched trowel, then press the mosaic on to it, with the paper side turned up.

11 Leave to dry for about 2 hours, then dampen the paper with a sponge and gently peel it away. Leave overnight for the adhesive to dry.

12 Grout the mosaic with more tile adhesive, using a grout spreader. Clean off any excess adhesive with a damp sponge and leave the mosaic to dry overnight.

13 Remove any remaining adhesive with abrasive paper (sandpaper). Alternatively, a sponge and dilute hydrochloric acid can be used, but you must wear goggles and rubber (latex) gloves, and apply it outside or where there is good ventilation.

14 Wash any acid residue from the surface with plenty of water and a large sponge. Finish the mosaic by polishing the surface with a dry, soft cloth. You should clean it from time to time with mild detergent and a coarse brush to remove moss and dirt.

China Tiles

If you would like to introduce mosaic to an outdoor setting but are daunted by a large project, these tiles are the perfect solution. They can be left freestanding, casually propped around the garden, or can be fixed to a wall as an eye-catching feature.

STEP 2

STEP 3

STEP 5

1 Prime the back of a plain ceramic tile with diluted PVA (white) glue using a paintbrush and leave to dry. Draw a simple, rough design on the back of the tile using a soft pencil.

2 Using tile nippers, cut a selection of coloured and patterned china into small pieces that will fit into your design and arrange them in groups according to their colour and shape.

3 Dip the tesserae into tile adhesive and press them, one by one, on to the tile, using the drawing as a guide. Make sure there is enough adhesive on the tesserae; when they are pressed on the tile, glue should ooze out around them. Cut more small pieces as necessary to fill the gaps.

4 When the tile is completely covered in mosaic, leave it overnight for the adhesive to set hard.

5 Mix acrylic paint or cement stain with the tile grout so that it goes effectively with the colours in your design. (It will be a little paler when dry.) Wearing rubber (latex) gloves, rub the grout into the surface of the mosaic with your fingers, ensuring all the gaps between the tesserae are filled. Leave to dry for 10 minutes.

6 Scrub the surface of the tile with a stiff nailbrush to remove all the excess grout. When clean, leave the tile to dry for 24 hours. Finish by polishing it with a dry, soft cloth. Repeat for any other tiles you want to make.

Polystyrene (Styrofoam)
or wooden spheres
PVA (white) glue
Paintbrush
Pencil
Selection of china
Mirror
Tile nippers
Tile adhesive
Vinyl matt emulsion (flat latex),
acrylic paint or cement stain
Tile grout
Rubber (latex) gloves
Nailbrush
Soft cloth

Decorative Spheres

These mosaic spheres can be used as unusual garden ornaments, perhaps grouped with plant pots, or you could fill a bowl with them to make a striking table centrepiece.

STEP 2

STEP 4

STEP 7

1 Seal the polystyrene (Styrofoam) or wooden spheres with a coat of diluted PVA (white) glue. Leave to dry.

2 Roughly draw a simple design on to each sphere using a pencil. A combination of circular motifs and stripes works well, but you can experiment with any geometric forms, or try abstract designs or simple organic shapes.

3 Cut the china and mirror into pieces using the tile nippers. Combine different sizes of tesserae to fit the design, but bear in mind that small pieces will be easier to stick on the curved surface of the spheres.

4 Stick the pieces to the spheres with tile adhesive, using enough to bed them in securely, cutting more to fill any gaps.

5 Leave the spheres overnight for the adhesive to harden.

6 Add a little coloured vinyl matt emulsion (flat latex), acrylic paint or cement stain to the tile grout, to achieve a colour that will complement the mosaic designs.

7 Wearing rubber (latex) gloves, rub the grout into the surface of each sphere, working it into the cracks between the tesserae with your fingers.

8 Leave for a few minutes until the surface has dried, then brush off any excess grout using a stiff nailbrush.

9 Leave to dry overnight, then polish with a dry, soft cloth. Allow the spheres to air for several days before you arrange them.

Ceramic mosaic tiles
in several colours
Tile nippers
Rubber (latex) gloves
Notched trowel
Tile adhesive
Terracotta planter
Putty knife
Tile grout
Acrylic paint or cement stain
Rubber grout spreader
Nailbrush
Soft cloth

Windowsill Planter

A terracotta planter can be embellished with pieces of tile, which are further enhanced by being grouted in a colour chosen to complement them. If the planter is frost-resistant, it can safely be left outdoors all year round.

STEP 2

STEP 3

STEP 4

1 Snip the tiles into small pieces using tile nippers. You will need a selection of small squares of a single colour to create the borders of the design, and random shapes in several different colours to fill the space between them.

2 Use the notched trowel to apply tile adhesive generously to the sides of the planter, working on one side at a time.

3 Using a putty knife, apply a small amount of tile adhesive to the back of each of the single-coloured square tesserae. Position them on the planter to form two straight lines parallel with the horizontal sides of the planter, making a border at the top and bottom edges of the side of the pot.

4 Fill in the central design in the same way with the randomly cut tesserae, mixing the colours to make an abstract design. Leave fairly large gaps of a consistent size between the tile pieces, as thick bands of coloured grout are part of the final design. Leave to dry for 24 hours.

5 Mix the grout with paint or cement stain. Using the rubber spreader, apply grout all over the surface of the planter, pressing right down between the tesserae. Wipe the spreader over the surface of the planter to make sure the grout is evenly applied. Allow the surface to dry.

6 Brush off any excess grout with a nailbrush, then leave to dry for 48 hours. Polish with a dry, soft cloth.

Shell Table

This simple small table top has been transformed with a shell mosaic to make a piece of furniture that would be perfect for a patio or conservatory. The symmetrical arrangement of the shells makes an eye-catching design.

STEP 1

STEP 2

STEP 3

1 Using a ruler, pencil, protractor and a pair of compasses, draw a geometric pattern on the table top, following the design shown or creating your own.

2 Using PVA (white) glue and a fine paintbrush, stick a scallop shell to the centre of the table. Glue pink shell pieces inside the starfish shape and surround the starfish with a circle of small snail shells.

3 Break up several sea urchins into tesserae of regular size using tile nippers, and glue them to form a circle outside the snail shells.

4 Glue ten scallop shells around the edge of the table top, spacing them evenly. Fill in the gaps between them with mussel shells. Glue cowrie shells in arches between the scallops.

STEP 4

STEP 5

5 Glue a limpet shell in the middle of each space in the inner circle. Fill in the spaces around the limpet shells in between the legs of the starfish and inside the snail shell circle with small cockle shells.

▶

STEP 6

STEP 7

STEP 8

6 Fill in the remaining spaces on the table top with an assortment of small shells arranged in a regular pattern.

7 Starting in the centre and working on only a small area at a time, spread tile grout over the surface of the mosaic. Use a grout spreader or small palette knife to press the grout into the gaps, or wear rubber (latex) gloves and use your fingers to work in the grout.

8 Use a paintbrush to work the grout into the smallest gaps and smooth the surface with a little water. Press firmly with a damp flannel (washcloth) to impact the grout around the shells. Rub the flannel over the shells in an outward direction to remove any grout from the surface of the shells.

9 Repeat steps 7–8 until you have grouted the whole mosaic. Leave to dry for several hours, then polish with a mop attachment on your drill or with a soft cloth.

10 Paint the grouting with diluted emulsion (latex) or watercolour paints: pale blue-green for the inner circle and outer edge, and pale ochre for the midway band. Finally, apply several coats of pale blue-green colourwash to the edge of the table top.

11 You could coat the table top with a matt or silk varnish to prevent spilt drinks from making stains. If you decide to leave it as it is, simply clean it from time to time with mild detergent and a stiff scrubbing brush or toothbrush.

STEP 9

STEP 10

Quick Tip
Keep the small shells to a regular size and height so that objects such as mugs and glasses will not wobble too much when placed on the table.

Fountain Bowl

This striking water feature is perfect for use outdoors on a patio or indoors in a conservatory. Being portable, it can be brought in and out of the garden and would make a perfect centrepiece.

STEP 1

STEP 2

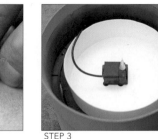
STEP 3

1 To make the stand, fix the wooden panel inside the dustbin by screwing through from the outside. Attach the wheeled feet to the blocks of wood and screw them to the underside of the wooden panel. Drill a hole near the base of the dustbin for the pump cable.

2 Using a hammer, flatten the piece of copper pipe at one end in order to create a narrow jet of water. Using the tip of a screwdriver, open up the flattened end of the copper pipe slightly to ensure that the water will flow freely.

3 Position the plastic container in the centre of the reservoir, resting on top of the wooden panel. Add the water pump, threading the cable through the hole drilled near the base of the reservoir in step 1.

4 Select glass mosaic tiles in a range of colours to achieve a bold, brightly coloured effect.

STEP 5

STEP 6

STEP 7

5 It is a good idea to test out the mosaic design on a piece of paper first. Arrange the tiles in concentric circles to achieve a pleasing blend of colours.

6 If necessary, cut some of the tiles into narrower pieces using the tile nippers.

7 Spray the outside of the fibreglass bowl with copper paint if desired. Leave to dry, then, starting at the rim of the bowl, apply two lines of glue from a glue gun, keeping a small gap between the lines.

8 Press each tile firmly on to the adhesive. When the first row of tiles is in place, follow the same procedure for the second row, and continue with each successive row until you reach the centre.

9 Finish by laying the final circle of tiles around the hole in the centre of the bowl. You may have to cut the tiles to fit the final row. Allow to dry overnight.

10 Spread tile grout between the tiles using the spreader. Allow to dry for 10 minutes, then wipe with a damp sponge. Fill the plastic container with water and position the bowl over the copper pipe.

11 Plug in the pump, then adjust its flow rate to create a range of different sounds, from gushing fountain to gentle trickle, depending on your mood. You can wheel the fountain to different positions in the conservatory or garden as you wish, but be careful to keep the power cable and plug clean and dry.

STEP 8

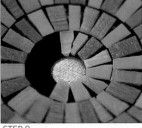

STEP 9

Quick Tip
The fountain is a striking modern feature in warm oranges and reds, but greys, blues and greens might suit a more traditional garden better.

Sea Urchin Garden Seat

Sea urchins are found clinging to wild, rocky shorelines or nestling in rock pools. This simple, pleasing shape inspired by their form will bring a hint of the ocean to your garden.

STEP 1

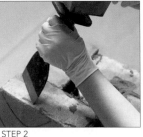
STEP 2

STEP 5

1 Mix 3 parts sand to 1 part cement with some water. Use this to assemble the breezeblocks (cinderblocks) into a cube by creating two L shapes with the cut block in the centre at the top.

2 When the mortar is dry, knock the corners off the blocks with a hammer and chisel. Continue to shape the blocks until the top part is fairly rounded.

3 Using charcoal, draw a curved line flowing around the four sides of the cube. Draw lines radiating out from the centre top and down over the sides. Lay out the tiles on the design to check the spacing.

4 Add a little black cement stain to the tile adhesive and trowel it directly on to the block, no more than 5mm (¼in) thick.

5 Place each tile on the surface of the adhesive and tap it down once sharply with the tile nippers. Do not adjust the tiles too much or they may not adhere.

6 Wrap the pieces of slate in a piece of sacking (heavy cloth) and hammer them into large pieces. Use one dark shade of tiles for the curved line marked in step 3. Place the slate pieces on the adhesive around the base of the seat and tap them down using the nippers.

7 In the gaps between the slate pieces on the square base of the seat, place glass baubles, silver and glass circles, blue and white cut tiles or stones in waves. Leave to dry completely. Grout the seat with more sand and cement mix (as in step 1). Allow to dry slowly and thoroughly before using.

Index